Anniversary

Richard W. Halperin

salmonpoetry

Published in 2010 by
Salmon Poetry
Cliffs of Moher, County Clare, Ireland
Website: www.salmonpoetry.com
Email: info@salmonpoetry.com

ISBN 978-1-907056-33-8

Cover artwork: Jessie Lendennie
Cover design & typesetting: *Siobhán Hutson*
Printed in England by imprint*digital*.net

For Kirsten

Acknowledgements

Acknowledgement is due to the editors of the following publications in which a number of these poems have appeared:

Cyphers, The Stinging Fly, THE SHOp: A Magazine of Poetry, Poetry Ireland Review, Revival Poetry Journal, The Stony Thursday Book (2007, 2008 and 2009), *Ropes Unravelled, Open Christianity Newsletter* (Ireland), *The Interpreter's House, Planet: The Welsh Internationalist, CrossWords: Anthology of Christian Poetry, Boomslang Poetry Magazine, First Time Magazine, Fuselit: Tilt, Obsessed with Pipework, 14 Magazine, The Delinquent* (UK), *Anon Poetry Magazine* (UK), *Orta Christmas Anthology* 2009, *Poetry on the Lake Journal One* (Italy), *Van Gogh's Ear, Disle* (France), *Descant* (Canada).

'For Victor Gollancz' won first prize in the Blue Butterfly Christian Poetry Competition 2007. 'Two of the Loveliest Words' and 'Diagonal House' were third-prize winners in respectively the Slipstream Open Poetry Competition 2009 and the Essex Poetry Competition 2007. Some poems were honourably mentioned and anthologized: 'Elgar' (Flarestack Competition 2009), 'Where does the soul go when it goes?' (Ver Poets Open Competition 2009), 'I am born' (Hastings International Poetry Competition 2009), 'Epithalamion from the Palisades' (Blue Butterfly, 2005). 'In the country' ('My dear Masha')and '18 February 2007' were long-listed in the Bridport Competition 2007.

Some poems were included in a public lecture 'Light in Religion, Science and Poetry, and a Piece of Broken Glass' given at Glenstal Abbey (Ireland) under the auspices of the Metanexus Foundation's Sophia Europa Project, co-ordinated by the University of Limerick.

Contents

Anniversary

You left your shawl on the chair.
I don't know what got into you.
You never do things like that.

I enter the room and there's the shawl.
In the morning the light hits it.

Part of the fringe touches the floor now.
It didn't used to.
Sometimes, I suppose, gravity pulls it.

Last night I thought I heard the chair say,
'How much longer? I'm not her shoulders.'
'No,' I said, 'you're not.'

In the morning, the weave catches the light,
when there is light.

'Doesn't this desk have a chair?' the mover asked, 'Did my
    buddy move it out?'
'No to the first,' I said.
'Oh,' he said. 'Good.'

The light hits the floor where the carpet was,
or the hole where the floor was.

You were always so careful about that shawl.
You never wanted it to brush the ground.

Why did you leave it on the chair then?
You never did things like that.

Concerning Divine Light

I saw it once as our boat approached Evian
We on the deck, boys diving off the pier
You too thin in a summer dress
The palm trees and casino sliding toward us
Lausanne the other shore sliding under us
The prow sliding through the penultimate miracle of blue.

'We don't need to come here,' you said, 'I've just been healed.'
'I know it,' I said, 'I can feel it.'

Then in the hotel you were sick again
though not so sick as two years later when you died.

But we had crumpled up shabby little death and shabby little courage
and tossed them over the side like garbage
because that's what they are in divine light.

January Fracture

The snow was falling like burnt roses
Your dog was running alongside you
Your cheeks and scarf and hat were apples in the wind
And there was no more park
And I could have killed your mother for any harm she
    might ever have done you
And all you cared about was your dog running
And I fell backwards
And there was no ground to break that fall
And I didn't even know who you were
Nor ever did nor could
And all the rest is words
But that was love.

Diagonal House

Of course the house is diagonal. Right over there. No one
even knows how it could be standing. No foundation,
   leans on point,
as it were, right off the ground, going thataway.

Of course, the ground could be diagonal and the house straight across,
it's hard to tell. Don't know how he can be living in it
   without falling
out a window, one day he might.

We see him in it walking about sometimes, or sometimes
just reading and a bit of writing. The curtains don't work right,
   they hang down straight,
so with the windows parallelograms it's not too hard to see in.

Works wonderfully in the rain, a diagonal house, no need of gutters,
   the rain slides
right off the roof, grey it is, used to be nut brown not so long ago.
We I mean we didn't mean to go on about one diagonal house.

Wonderful
the way it points up away from or maybe points down into, it's
   hard to tell.
Well, no matter what, you've got to say diagonal's got its
   good points,

for one thing with all that air and light freed up beneath it,
   it's lovely for
the rabbits, gives them more of a chance to scamper. Well,
   all we meant to say is, it's a
diagonal house, right over there.

The Thought of You

'This is the tale I pray the divine muse to unfold to us. Begin it, goddess, at whatever point you will.'

The Odyssey, trans. E.V. Rieu

I should have jotted it down when the goddess came

I thought poetry was something that only happened to other people
so I continued on my way to shop
to buy something that reminded me of you
and I bought it
and now I own it
and so I lost you
all over again

Epithalamion from the Palisades

Kyrie bless our marriage reft
I the half two do ask you to retune return her
Rent rose ash
Slapped twisted
Tristed
Early out of
Newtonian time and tense. In out I saw she was on off zero

+ plus, her cross crossed, her pulse repulsed radiant in

Rivers rained down to Kingdom's tented grounds where
I AM reigns. There
Campground receives all. Kyrie this day bless. You who
Hard prest the grin groan grain grace of her groom me for grist
As marriage balm.
Remelt the smelt of her as lo the
Dear bride's changed to bird in eyeblink's twink one two three

4. Therefore

Eléison Kyrie. Eléison Criste our now only
Verb. Glory us to that morning that
Even now is left: our lovely
Rest. Bless this marriage.

A good thick poem

Blue guitars and thin gold birds do what for whom?
The last thing eternity needs is an interior decorator.

I want to know. I want a good fat stunted poem,
plaintalk and drool weaving like a drunk across a tennis court.

Talk at me. Am I loved?   Where did she go? What should I do?
Who killed hope in the parlour with a gun? Colonel Mustard?

Answer me so I won't forget.
Club me with it so I never have to read again.

'Well, Madam, he's dead in the library all right.
Only a good thick poem could have done that.'

The Chair

In a house not mine, the owners away,
On a day like any other although all days are different,
I sank as one sometimes does en route
Into the gentle grave gravity of an accidental chair
Whose occupation was to be there,
And as I sank, the precincts of my mind lifted off and fell
Like a tent from the pull of ropes and guys,
Although all ropes are different,
And there was something sat in the chair, I away,
And for five minutes without ceasing,
Although the sixth minute was like any other,
The something sitting in the chair
Banged its fists against the arms
And stamped its feet upon the floor not mine
And, in my chair, cried and cried like a baby.

With how sad steps, O Moon, you

May moon, you venerable bead, now breathe
her back or inhale me. May your white clot
clasp her caved chest, her chirps choked on death's cot
clear to the Sea of Tranquillity. Breathe
for her, old poached pear. A midwife slap. Breathe
her coughed past merciless light where she not
she but something brighter, laughs. Then, argonaut
moon, turn, return to take me up who breathe

here lying beached in gasps on this sestet.

Letter to My father

Well, here I am. I have the Toscanini records, the fishing rod,
the size 11 shoes, the photo of an old man in a straw hat
(not you, me, but it's the same photo), the Marx Brothers jokes,
the bitterness, the let's call it panic, the one side of the mouth
    turned down,
the same crap printed in the same Sunday papers,
the wet kisses never delivered an eye twinkle serving as the
    great code,
the complete works of Somerset Maugham 'The Verger' still
    the favourite,
the glass of milk with the steak and the chocolate pie,
everything, in fact, for Sunday evening when you had custody
    of me,
except where the hell are you Daddy?

The wind blew gently through the house

The wind blew gently through the house
ruffling the pages of the books we had not read
and familiar books. The wind blew gently, coaxing pictures

off the walls and photographs out of wallets. The wind lifted gently
the outrageous puns in the kitchen, the winestains left by guests,
the guests, cousin Edwin in his chair, the ruby star

pasted to the forehead of the birthday girl,
you and me in the yard all those evenings, the dog Buffy
under the yard, worlds within worlds, the death of hope,

the oak armoire, and all the tattered stars. And we had learned
    in school
that a pound of feathers and a pound of lead weigh the same
    or barely,
and the wind blew gently through the house.

And if my sister

And if my sister kills again,
well, she does things like that.

And if my sister remembers who I am,
she's having a good day.

And if my sister shoplifts,
nobody has a better right.

And if my sister wants to make love to me,
I keep letting her.

And if my sister runs off with umpteen losers,
that's my sister for you.

And if my sister finally breaks my heart,
I forgive her.

But if my sister is God,
I have to think about it.

Grey Cat in Red Boots

How do you know he's not resurrection?
How do you know he's in the room?
How do you know he's not in the room?
How do you know what a room is?
If you had just stepped daintily out of death,
what would you look like?
Appearances are deceptive.
So are disappearances.

We've all seen death.
In the middle of a gesture, no gesture.
In the middle of a life, no life.
The clock stops.
I sometimes think if one awakes
it must be where there are no clocks.

Someone sent me today
a postcard of a grey cat in red boots.
Rampant, prancing in a grey room.
A red thread in one raised front paw.

Blue wouldn't have done it.
Pie in the sky.
But red.
Why not?

Everything else gunmetal grey.

It's a question of waiting
for the right kind of screw to be loose.

Old Lady in Red Hat

She walks in dignity.
Summer blaze. Park.
The sun hits the path, the hat,
not her. She did not choose to be old,
but she could choose a hat,
and did. Cotton, cheap, squashable
(not yet). Red shadows and motes
move round her in cortege where before,
red wasn't.
She's had her day. Is still having it.
Who are you, lady? Who will you be?

Very Orange Sun on the Horizon

You were very sleepy.
What better, then, than to sleep?

You were no longer hungry
but they tried to feed you,

a little jellied water
on a sponge.

I thought that I could hear—and you?—
a rush of souls coming in and going out.

A perfect understanding between us,
and an ending. You coalesced.

'It's the end of the trail,'
you'd said, much earlier.

I'd slammed that remark against
the cheap Technicolor wall

of all the westerns of my youth,
to make it part of fake fate.

You were very sleepy, and now I am, too.
The road sign that you saw

I see, through the painted dust:
'What larks! What hell!'

Is this where I came in? Save my seat?
One of these two, surely.

Blue Pane

Temples were stone once but no glass.
Then sand, sun, focus, luck, ingenuity: glass.
Coloured only, no such thing as clear.

Not just temple now:
synagogue, mosque, church,
pub, bank, cinema,
requiring, for certains it seems,
yes, that necessary glass.
Don't know in which I was.
Not mourning. That was past.

Looked without seeing.
Struck sane. A blue pane.
(Now can't find it.)
You behind it.

I didn't think I could be this kind of happy, my dear, ever again

A nervous woman and a solid block of blue
sea. The sea twittered, the woman waited,
the sun promised nothing. 'I thought I was just born,'
she said, 'yet I watch in a wheelchair. What happened
   in-between?'
A dog ran along the shore. 'Emery,' the woman said. 'My dog.'
'Never yours, let's be clear about that,' said the dog.
'I was what love is,' then cut out over the solid blue
to behind the sun. 'Why no one else?' she said to no one else.
'Surely I loved my husband, my child, my par-ee-ants more.'

The sea twittered, the woman waited.

'Why my dog?' 'Arf,' Emery corrected. 'Why Emery?' she said.
'I was four when I got him.' 'Arf,' Emery corrected.
'When we were,' she said.
'Do we only have here the one we loved the bestiest,
   just the one?
Or the one that loved us the very bestiest?
You'd have thought Susan would have been someone here now.'

'Arf,' something said.

'Well,' she said, 'I've plenty of time to think about it.'

Two old ladies were walking hand in hand toward the river

I have had no inspiration for oh my such a long time now
so I have made a poem out of nothing:

Two old ladies were walking hand in hand toward the river.

The moon—it was a half moon—was shining
on two old ladies walking hand in hand toward the river.

Whatever are you doing?

Are you talking to me?
or are you talking to the two old ladies walking hand in
   hand toward the river?
It is so cold, though.

Yes, do you mean the half moon is so cold? or the river is so cold?

I do. It is very cold, the half moon in the river.

You mean, the reflection of the half moon in the river.

I saw what I saw.
The half moon is in the river.
The two old ladies walking hand in hand are in the river,
they are not walking toward it any more.

I don't see two old ladies in the river, I don't see the half moon,
only a sky with no moon and a riverbank and a river flowing.

Nor I. Nothing up there and nothing in there. So we agree.

Do you mean, with your two old ladies, the soul and the body?
Do you mean the baby who just died?

Do you mean Beethoven on his deathbed?
Do you mean my father who did die, and that a long time ago?
Do you mean the ladybird I just stepped on?
Do you mean the breath I just took?
And why a half moon?

Yes, I do.
I am describing walking toward being made out of nothing
and it's easier to take if I tell you it's a poem.

Even the dying light

Even the dying light is light. Even
Love's last molecule before indifference
Begins is love. Even warped sense is sense.
Immense the nouns. Immense their tense. Years happen,
And adjectives wash away. At the end,
Not, I was happy; but, I was. Not, she
Was radiant; but, she. I, she, we—lovely
Without lovely. And adverbs—our big pretend:
He thought well, he thought dully; the miracle
Is, he thought. The miracle is, he wept;
Not he barely wept, or wretchedly. Who,
What, not when; is, loves, finds, not how—these buckle
The spectacle. Beautiful you, decrepit
You, is you. You! Even dead you is you.

Rue de Bellechasse

This is the street and this the place
when I last saw you. You were wearing
your Venice dress, white muslin
with garnet ribbons at the wide square neck,
your black hair loose and curly, your easy stride,
your ankles, always too thin, sandals
of some sort, a silk shawl not worn but lightly carried
for when evening came, because it gets cold
in Venice in the evening. That's it. A picture.
You coming toward me, that smile,
clearly something you were dying to tell me
and were about to. The natural swing of things,
missing from most of those paintings from
the Cinquecento at the Louvre—moments, yes,
but not the natural swing of things. Corner
of the rue Las Cases just by the little grocery shop.
You'd died three months before, but then,
you'd never cared much about details.

The Book

Sometimes, rarely, a book opens the book.
Pip and Estella, a seed and a star.
The sides of the barrel rot.
The Thames disappears round a corner.

Seven days are a waste of one's attention
Which is why Moses dispenses with them quickly.
On the eighth day, and there is yet no ninth,
God revulsed the heavens and the earth.
And all was void
As science so well sees.

Sometimes, rarely, a book opens the book.
Plato's cave.
Pip and Estella.
Some remarks of Jesus.
The sides of the barrel fall away.
Justice and his idiot brother revenge disappear round a corner.
One stands upon the void and is the void.

Except, in one's hand, the handkerchief of a book.
A seed and a star.

For Victor Gollancz

I praise the foundation of the earth and its four corners
I praise the spaces between words, because there the Spirit moves
I praise birds for their crazy loquacity
I praise fowls that cannot fly, because they are signs
I praise trees, the birch and the oak, the leaves and the lungs
I praise streams for their brevity
I praise puddles, because few do
I praise the reliability of the morning, the fate of the evening
I praise the gopher for scratching its head
I praise fishes for the beauty of their obliviousness
I praise dirt because it is we before God breathed
I praise the rat, the rose, the rooster, the rain, the roach,
    because they are not we
I praise neither the beginning nor the end but the middle
I praise the door in and the door out of the vast invisible House
I praise the capacity for praise which is left when all else isn't
I pray not to see but to notice
    the pauses between pains
    the gasps between evils
    the gaps in the grandeur
    the glints in the grunts
    the hiccup in the prayer
Which is all God hears
As praise.

Sparks among the Stubble

I remember when you were beautiful
I remember when you were
I remember when you
I remember you
I ember you
Ember you
Ember
You
You ember
You I ember
You I remember
You I remember when
You I remember when you were
You I remember when you were beautiful
You I remember when you were beautiful when you were
You
You I
You I remember

Peristalsis

For Elizabeth

The clock goes clockwise
It doesn't go back

The heart goes heartwise
One two one two

Peristalsis goes forward forward
To end in muck

Waiting is moving toward
Until accident snuffs out precedent

Everything of course moves on or isn't
Only one gear till the car gets clamped
Only one theorem possible for the forum

Anti-thus,
After isn't
Sometimes I sit in a garden we once sat in
    Stephen's Green   Les Tuileries   Central Park El Retiro

Sometimes there
The heart does beat backwards
Two one two one

And proves
To logicians
The miracle

July

He went swimming with his mates and never came back.
No one remembers the expedition now.
Long time ago.
Everyone was twelve, shouting, splashing.
Dripping wet on shore, shiny.
'Hi Larry where ya hiding?'

Haven't thought of it in donkey's years.
Good question.

Poppies

Poppies hang on to each other to keep from being blown away they
just for a split second criss-cross tendrils weave in the
wind hook their heads about their mates they throw their
fraction of an ounce around trying with everything they've got as
that damned wind as that damned win keeps coming and
poppies and poppies and poppies and poppies are not the only ones.

Polly

Polly wants a cracker, says Sylvia Plath.
Polly wants to know what's going on.
Polly wants a nice slice of peace.
Polly doesn't want to cease.
Or does Polly?
Pretty Polly pease porridge any temperature will do.
Hello you.
Polly wants affection.
Polly wants dissection.
Polly wants a cracker.
Polly wants a cracker.
Polly wants a cracker
In the worst way.

Greystones Bray Walk

The tug of the soul like a fish at the end of a line

I but who am I as I walk on the edge of the sea
The Irish Sea someone calls it but the sea has no name
A name is like knitting a red hat to put on, well, the sea
The tug of your hand in mine as I walk on the edge of

Tug, tug, there is weight in my hand, and flesh, and bone,
    and gristle,
But is that not the
Is that not the weight in my hand of a shout of wind
    gusting from Wales
But what is wind the wind has no name nor should it nor
    should Wales

As the DART clicks by and the Brent geese rise and two
    dogs splash and the wind
Burns into my face and my red windbreaker is only red
    over fat and flesh
And my soul tugs at me from the east—but should not
    that be west?—
And the wind is burning my eyes to salt and my hand is
Blinded by a tensile ball of light but what is a hand
And to say your name would be as ridiculous as to say
    Irish Sea
And the red hat of the day blows off. 'Almost there,'
    my pal cries ahead of me, 'Bray!'

In a Hotel on Eustace Street

A filthy pane
Some unfinished construction outside
Rooftops a grey Dublin day
My view from a hotel on Eustace Street
Another stop on my pilgrimage.

Last night a party in the suburbs.
A daughter of the house in her clear soprano voice
Sings 'Bist du bei mir' which she had just learned
The week before for a friend's wedding. Troubled
By the song's beauty, she feels she must explain afterwards
And does: 'I don't believe in God. I'm a humanist.'

Fair enough.

In my friendly shabby rented cubicle
On Eustace Street more or less
I wake up this morning by the grace of
And go downstairs for Full Irish Breakfast
In my case coffee and one soft-boiled egg
        who in life had every reason to be suspicious
        and whom I can barely look in the face.

After, I walk a few streets of Temple Bar that was.
I walk from Dame Street to the Liffey and back again
        glitz   guilt   gilt   the baby with the bathwater
        the new Dublin

I cross Dame Street for South Great Georges Street.
On one side I hear Trinity: 'I'm a humanist.'
On the other side I hear Christ Church: 'I'm empty.'

In the middle I hear my tripes: 'Coffee's kicked in,
Back to the hotel.'

In my hotel on Eustace Street
On my cot at 11:00 AM
I try to digest my last twenty-four hours since Paris.
The sun breaks out over the scaffolding on the roof across.
An empty-handed magpie flies past on this Bank Holiday.
I'm fading fast into a nap
Whatever a nap is.

I miss being on my back on the flat flat desert near Jeddeh
With its night bowl of stars
  no churches no mosques no humanism
  no religion no nations only praise for

Where Bach was when he heard and sketched I AM WHO AM
Into a tune.
Where errant souls feel to flock.

In a hotel on Eustace Street
Nap closing in
I salute my so-called dead
And the so-called alive
And the ridiculous bravery of brevity.
I salute the clues and comforts of certain tunes.
I salute I AM WHO may AM in the souls of searchers.
I salute a filthy pane
Some unfinished construction outside.

The Halt

Sunday, 6th July. Must be brief. Exhausted after this leg.
Mrs Ruisdale out looking at cows. The Cobben boy
obsessed by balloons. Has no father. (Dead at sea?
Must check.) Curtains mildewed. Or nightshirt?
(Must check in morning.) Millet field, quite blood red
in sunset. On fire? Can't be. Maybe the hills.

Edwina still dead. Un-
believable, really.
Wildly despondent in coach. No one noticed.

One thought per entry. So: The Bible and Mosquitoes:
Little horrors. Has anyone noticed?—
the Bible if you slog it out. Even Chronicles.
Sometime years later—the halt before this one—
the world makes a gigantic adjustment to it. Thud.
Not vice-versa. The world to *it*. Flew right into my ear the
little bastard the whole night. Then, thud, it was correct—
that we have open flapless ears and mosquitoes.
Thank you, Bibes.

Continue in the morning. Just that.

She was in no hurry

I saw a woman walking in a field of rye.
She was in no hurry. A child was at her side, a little boy.
Hatless, she showed no fear of the sun at noon, but, I thought, she's
Headed for the shade, and that explains it. I'd never noted
Until then that rye moves in waves, brown, yellow, green, glints of white.
How like a beach it was, how like—it was—what cities aren't:
Waves undulating or maybe it was she that was the waves.
Her easy walking. The boy grabbed her sunburnt hand and kissed it.
Who wouldn't have? on such a day as this of air and almost quiet,
And rustles in the brush of mice and moles and grasshoppers and grain.
I thought she was coming toward me, boy in tow—but as I gazed,
She walked farther. Does the soul really look like that? Oh, yes.
I knew: it was she. (I wouldn't have thought that, but for the moles.)
But having fallen in love with you the day before, I barely noticed.

Masha

i. In the country

The days pass quickly in the country.
My friend is sleeping in the long grass. The sun strikes the picnic table
with the faded checked cloth, and I write you, my dear Masha,
because why not? I remember when we played duets at the piano,
you playing and singing, I listening, three make a duet my dear Masha,
as you now know, I too one day. It is good here, it might be the time
of George Eliot and Turgenev, it might be two minutes ago before
I thought of you this time again. The sun is setting across the mountains,
their name is irrelevant, and I am using my best composition book style
to hide myself, as it were, in a novel or classic, as my friend sleeps
in the long grass like an old yellow dog and will shake himself
and wake up soon, as I hope I will, my dear Masha,
but I too have to sleep first before that, like powder in the long grass,
long after this day is blown away, and then it will be, I hope,
we all in the country again, playing duets the three of us,
but I must stop writing now, before I clench anything
and spoil the flow of my composition book. And so it is evening now,
and I go inside the cottage to turn on my lamp, my friend already
in the kitchen. Click I try to go, but I see nothing but black.
'Ah,' says the lamp, 'I too used to work.' Time for tea now.

ii. Two of the loveliest words

And when we set off for the country, Papa, you cannot imagine
our excitement. We could not keep the children quiet, nor ourselves.
And when we arrived, you cannot imagine our despair.
Such a change from the old days! I don't know what was saddest—
that you weren't there still, or that you were but we couldn't find you.
Then the dog, tail wagging, went missing, into the lake, we think.
Then Pauline, who, however, had waved to us cheerfully first.
Then I myself never came back—from where?—and someone

called the police who, however, only left a recording
'We've gone to the country today; as it is Sunday, please call
your family doctor, here is the number.' And I thought to myself,
we need someone to translate this the way Constance Garnett—
aren't they two of the loveliest words in the language?
I meditate upon them—opened up the Russians to us.
Because we cannot read without that, only the memory of the heart,
only a scattering of place-names, but not, for instance, why did we set off,
and why were we already there, and who, exactly, are you, Papa?

iii. Sligo on a Summer Night

Let the knitting drop from your hands, the cat
will play with it for a while, her hands are
not so gnarled. I know you've said
that when the hands are busy
the mind is free; but the mind cannot see
very far like that.

Look over the hills, you can catch
the reflection of the ocean
in the nimbus clouds. You can see
the little sailboats and their crews
go down like broken matchsticks,
foam cover solid over
as if nothing had ever been;
but something had—

like the loose vest you were working
before the cat got it
and it was again as it
had always only ever been.

The house is creaking, the maybugs are hovering
now that twilight finally has come,
and—you can hear it? yes?—
the enormous click from under or above.

As if we outdoors of this house,
on this grass, with this evening;
as if the floating continents and every
last small star; as if all—all—
were in company
of the brightly painted gods and ancestors,
who do not need a nimbus by which to stare directly
at crews and sails and cries and the
voracious gulls; as if we all—all—
were in a tiny mamushka doll,
then clicked into a bigger mamushka
that we can't see, then into a bigger one than that,
then into a bigger one than that,

whether the larger mamushkas
are brighter or paler, or stronger or more cracked,
whether the painted red smiles are prettier
or more voracious, whether the hands
painted to the plump sides stay there
or extend—to pull us by our own hands,
which are not painted to our sides
and which are raised and reaching
to where the mind really breaks free,
and where there is—can you hear it?
yes? no? but you have dropped your knitting—
a kind heart beating.

Presence

When I shut my eyes I see you
When I close my ears I hear you
When I miss a train you're on it
When I catch my breath you are it
When I'm asked my name and go blank
I say yours.

Matchbox

The Chinese did not invent firecrackers, God is one.
Something is always being blown to bits,
everything gets blown to bits sooner or later, boo hoo.

But there's more than that,
as every dragon knew when there were dragons.

Nothing can also be blown to bits, something improbable triggers it,
and then instead of nothing—
love it's called.

In this room

In this room
I desired with desire
that you be

in this room.
In this room
you willed with will
to stay. In this

room
you saw with sight
no walls.

I barred with bars
this room
but you left
with leaves.

This room stopped
when you stopped
in this room
too long ago
to long.

In this room
now
there is no in
only
no
no will, sight, leaves, bar

yet in this room
of no
you are.

Last Lullaby

Your skin is soft
as tears
Your mouth is calm
with trust
your eyes are full
from time
Your ears are turns
of tunes
Your feet are flowers,
are tufts
So, hush.

The more you fear,
you float
The more you wake,
you dream
The more you sink,
you sing
The more you seem,
you hum
The more you're far
You were
So, hush.

Count the stars,
they're yours
Climb the stairs,
they're His
Leave the stains,
they're theirs
Lift the sails,
they're ours
Lose the storms,
they're mine
So, hush.

Soft now
Full now
Tuft now
So, home

Crab Nebula

Never would I come to that stream
Never would I come to lose you

Never would I let you near that stream

You in a white shirtdress that day
(And how many days before)
Running toward me
But walking backwards really
(Slowly it looked to me)

Retreating as if advancing
Dead as if dancing
Mercury not mine
Toward a hundred million million stars
You the greater radiant

Until there was no more shore
No more before
Nor you
Nor trace of alleluia

Except that stream stream stream stream stream
And 'Hellogoodbye. Fooled ya.'

Which is why
Never would I let you near that stream
Never would I come to lose you.

Sir Philip Sidney

Sir Philip Sidney
Had a kidney
Chop chop chop

Emily Brontë
Had bad bronchi
Chop chop chop

Cover your fronts!
Cover your backs!
Humans have Art
But Time's got an ax
Chop chop chop

Vesak

This is not a poem.

You disappeared
The night of the full moon in May.
Vesak:
The birthday and enlightenment of the Buddha, they say.
The full moon every May.

You disappeared in hospital.
The day after Vesak 2003 was morgue day.

About the sky:
All one knows of the why of the sky is the moon.
Why? because we can only know the Other
Through some remnant of ourselves
(If Berkeley was right),
And the moon is ourselves, it came from earth.
In fact, it is part of us, promoted;
As you were promoted on Vesak.
The moon has a human face not from accident
But from incident.

The milk of the moon is therefore comfort
To those who look often at the sky.

One may in fact often see
In a May sky—
Or at the other end of the balance,
November when souls frankly prance—
A grin without a moon.

Meow.

Whatever one sees
(If Berkeley is right)
Is.
Is
Is the only comfort a watcher
Has.

One may think the full moon disappears
All but one day a month.
But it doesn't.
If one has very good night vision, one can see it.
The full moon always only is.

That is why
This is not a poem.

17 October 1997

A temple there was
On the isle of Miyajima
A girl walking in that temple
A girl in a red cape.

A gate there was
Off the isle of Miyajima
A huge orange gate in the sea just offshore
Built hundreds of years ago
For the Buddha to enter through
Or to leave through.
He had always just been passing through
In his saffron robes,
And on that day, too.

Small suspicious sacred deer there were
On the isle of Miyajima
Deer walking about anywhere,
In their tender brown coats,
Watching tourists try to coax
Cans of iced coffee from the vending machines
That had been placed ubiquitous
On the isle
In case tourists in case a girl in case the Buddha
Irritable from the migrainous dirty air
Blown daily across the isle of Miyajima
From the neighbouring town of Hiroshima
Might want the kind of quick comfort
That only coins can buy.

A theatre there was at the edge
Of the isle of Miyajima
Planked floors a roof no walls,
Sea and the Buddha's great gate visible beyond.

The first Noh theatre,
Built for the Buddha or for a girl or for the deer or for tourists
Who might wish to see there
In open air by sea
Sacred imitations of the sacred,
Which was what theatre had meant
In those days,
And on that day, too.

Into that theatre
Onto the smooth planks
Walked the girl there was
In a red cape—
Come from the temple the coffee cans the tourists the deer
A girl who
Always sensitive to the sacred
Stood
Just stood,
One deer near her
A deer in a tender saffron coat.

A girl there was
Who stood
Just stood
On that day
By that deer
On the isle of Miyajima
By the town of Hiroshima
By a very big gate.

What do I almost remember?

In the hidden corridors of the mind, a trickle.
What do I almost remember? A silver perch on a line?

No, not that, I saw that when I was ten.
Some phrase I missed in Ecclesiastes, a flash of silver?

No, not that either. I was writing in Andrew's house,
on the big wooden table, motes in the air,

Toronto light, a big plain room, my hand
moving over a sheet of paper, a Greek book

nearby, Euripides, 'nothing so foul it isn't
washed clean by the sea,' curtains blowing in the breeze,

a poem about you spreading out over the page
like foam of the Aegean over sand, a trickle.

Was it 'no, I don't want to be born?' just before I was?
No, that I clearly remember.   'Let's keep talking,

I don't have to go home yet' (you, that first afternoon)?
No, I knew as the foam ran past my fingers

that that's what I'd heard that had made me
decide not to come out stillborn.

Your last words 'you were kind and competent
and that's what counts'?   No, none of these remembereds,

though they flash at a distance. 'In whose mind, then,
the trickle?' Ah, the better question.

Of course you

Of course you dreamed me. First, the top
Of the hill, the grass, the scorched path,
The yellow sun. Then, an old man
Descending, carefully, on a pony.
A knock on the wall, hard—are we
In a room? whose?—and Shelley is drowning
In the lake. The smell of the hill,
The tufts of parched grass, the wind ruffling
The pony's mane, the veined hands
Of the old man, not attending to the pony,
A girl child leading them, so gently.
Had there really been all that pain?
Had it really been worth it? And
There is Shelley engrossed, lying on
His stomach in the grass by the shore,
Reading some tract or other; so, that,
Or the other, was a rumour.
Then, the sun (it was noon) slid down
The cheek of the sky like a teardrop.
It was hard to believe that that
Could make the bright blue bluer, but it did.
You had always known, to comfort
Was at the heart of love. But for some of us,
The knowledge takes longer.

Apocrypha

Beloved,
don't expect a letter from me,
not from Patmos, not to Corinth.
You are the envelope, the letter is in you,
you have written it in expectation.
What did you hope I would write you?
What did you hope I would counsel you?
How badly did you hope I would miss you?
Here, I shall help you find it,
under your ribs. It is sodden,
it is shameful, it is stamped all over
with the stamp 'Rejected by Experts,'
it is, in fact, like mine
crushed into a ball under my own ribs.
Love is bad guesses
sent unerringly of themselves.
What need have we, then, of letters?

Crow black

Mouse brown is orange;
Coal black is blue;
Faces are acts of courage;
Crow black is purple and green;
If you look hard enough.

With no hard feelings

You visited me last night through the Gate of Horn.
You told me, 'Write a poem, you've been writing too many lately
and some not up to Paul's standard, but here's a good one,'
and you gave me the secret of it so that the words—
always reluctant children and worse at night—
would come easily. 'Wake up and write,' you said.

Your face was like a baby's, as it had been at the end,
and you crouched easily in a loose-fitting suit,
brown it seemed, like the Chinese wear
and as you sometimes preferred since one can move easily—
as you did, back into the darker brown of my brain and out,
with no hard feelings, as is your wont
when I capital J capital C Just Can't do something.
'It's too dour,' I thought to you (since this was all in thoughts)
and you shrugged a smile and waved

and left. Hours later, during coffee, it all came back,
and I looked by the bed to see if there was a hair left there
or a turned page, as some pilgrims or Homer have reported
after dreams, but there wasn't.

So this Sunday began, as Sundays do, with that there is
anything at all. Then in the middle of not much,
the gist returned. But I JC, so (another) mental note will do:

'Death is being picked up and having your brains
dashed out against the rocks. And praise for that.'
Or something like that.

The Cloche Hat

My mother looked good in them.
So, she wore them. When she walked
Out on my father, she bought
A new one, green like the woman's
With the green sunshade in the
National Gallery.

One Saturday shortly after, we
Had our photo taken at the Museum
Of Science and Industry,
Antique car wing. There we are,
In the front leather seat of
A Model A Ford. Behind
The steering wheel, I; looking out
Straight ahead, the Little Man
In neat serge. She at my side
In her cloche hat, prettier
Than Maureen O'Sullivan.

Plenty happened to us later, but
We'll well hide that under
A green sunshade, since I was
Brought up a gentleman; she, too.
God grant you such shade, reader.

Now, when I come across that
Photo, stiff and chipped with time,
I think we were never better
Than that, we two: side by side
Together in a front seat,
Going nowhere, green shade waiting.

A pretty white dress

A pretty white dress with some flowers on it
you looked so pretty in it
you showed up in it one day

I had been playing with a coffee spoon
the heat was bouncing off the sidewalk
my glasses sweating off my nose
the waiter, into making it in New York,
had left the table off the leash

You turned the street corner
'Hi,' you said,
and Third Avenue might have been Venice,
light bouncing everywhere.
'Hi,' I said, and the eternal conversation went on.
'Bye,' you said, 'Gotta go.'

Today

in a shop window in Paris
a pretty white dress
a few ounces of muslin, some coloured ribbons on it
like a bubble blown
from the Family Circle of the Old Met

Someone will look so pretty in it

'Hi,' I said, 'and good luck to you this day.'

Café Girl

'Welcome to Patmos,' she said.
'This is Paris,' I said.

'You're half-right,' she said.
'See that bozo over there
with the white wool hair
and the fine brass feet?
He's furious.'

'Why?'
'Postal strike,' she said.
'His letter with the seals
never got delivered.'

'I'll have another espresso then,' I said.
'Stronger and shorter.'
'That's my prayer for life on earth,' she said.

'You wouldn't be my wife at 20?' I said,
'You wouldn't be some version of me, now would you?'

'You must be a Jungie,' she said.
'You didn't answer my question,' I said.

'You don't miss much,' she said.
'This espresso's not much,' I said.

'Your poem's not much,' she said.
'You're not much,' I said.

'Right,' she said.
'Hardly anything of me at all.'

And there wasn't.

Portrait of a Portrait of My Wife

Done in Provincetown in 1967 by her boyfriend at the time,
In four pastels on grey paper.

The planes of her face, the movement of his hand
(Two masters always, the drawn and the drawer),
A spot of light—hers? his? difficult to tell with portraits—
Just outside the frame.

Green chalk on grey paper, yellow chalk, red chalk, white chalk
Smeared together to make
The line of a cheek, the brown of a jumper, the russet of hair,
Eyes—hers but whose now?—wide and calm,
As befits grey paper and an hour in Provincetown stolen from
The Master of light. A portrait of not yet my wife.

The poise of the head—hers to this day.
The stroke of the hand—his that day.
The eye of the viewer—mine, not yet twisted away, today.
And a spot of light just outside the frame, where
Poise, hand, eye coincide.

This although the bride
Is long since smashed and hurled
Into green, yellow, red, white elementals,
And no one can make a portrait of that picture.

So, an aged blob staring in a chair,
A rectangle on the wall opposite,
A spot in-between.
A room in slabs of colours and light, held in an equation:

A girl's face, brought into being
By the hand and love of an important
Boyfriend,
And an old man's thanks for that, make
The portrait of not yet my wife the portrait of my wife.
Alleluia.

18 February 2007

A man or less than that sits in his room
at nightfall, parachutefall, folds of silk

settling around his ankles, the plane gone
the pilot irrelevant.   He listens

to Strauss sung by Lisa Della Casa,
silver voice silver music written when

there were and there were extermination
camps. *Capriccio* and skulls, a century

folds in around the ankles of a man
lucky enough to have a room. Night rises

on the pegs of the voice of Della Casa,
whom, quite real, he heard once in New York

when almost everyone was still alive.
A man in his chair, and death or less than that.

O Lookingglass Land!

A landscape sheeped with dots
Verb in a pinafore
A lass that side of loss
Our world, less or more

Black swan white swan

An excavation made in 1975, behind the town of Vedbaek in Denmark revealed the body of a tiny child laid to rest in the embrace of a swan's wing. Next to the skeleton was the grave of the child's young mother, dead in childbirth . . . ; her face had been dusted with red ochre, the better to seem alive. Mother and child had been interred around 4800 BC.

(News clipping 2004)

Black swan white swan
bear my child
higher and higher
to the isle
past the last star's dial
winkless
Black swan white swan

Black swan white swan
bear my child
in steep sleep unreconciled
past the snares we defile
past our pile
to the isle
brinkless
live child dead child
Black swan white swan

Black swan white swan
bear my child
higher and higher
to the isle
live child dead child live child
linkless
Black swan white swan

Black swan white swan
bear my child
past the circles wild and mild
higher and higher
black swan white swan black swan
inkless
swanchild childswan one
my child my swan
Black swan white swan gone

A Child's Blue Christmas in Wales

There you are. You were describing
To friends 'A Child's Christmas in Wales.'
I sat down at the table, a friend introduced me,
You oblivious continued.
The book was no book, but a bubble of love,
We all in it, and Jesus, winter sinusitis,
Pure wonder, Wales and Bronx blizzards,
Hot coffee and cinnamon, a college cafeteria,
An eternal *thing* written in our own lifetime, a child,
A nineteen year-old girl explaining.
The tenderness of it—Christmas!—
Amid the clank of flatware, the smell of bluefish,
Smashed boysenberry pie, piles of cigarette butts,
The noise of drunks and angels—Christmas!
I knew then that one could know love
Just from hearing someone talking
About not whom but what she loved.
No candleflame could leap more
Brightly than the love of that book.
When love, the *thing* of it, is there, love leaps.
Thus, the next forty years of what
We came to call *us*.   This afternoon
I thought to ask you something about
'A Child's Christmas in Wales'
But you weren't around. You live on the blue star now.

Bedtime

'Tell me a story,' I said. 'I'm not sleepy.'

'But, my darling, why should I tell you one?
The birds sing and an old man hides his money
And the girl in the wrong shoes gets lost in the forest
And the little piglet climbs up to the stars
And the stag with the fuzzy antlers gets set upon by dogs
And the whole castle sinks into the sand
And somewhere a mother is crying, maybe me,
And it was you who gave the girl the wrong shoes, my darling,
And it is you who are climbing up to the stars
And there's no thread to these so I can't make a story
Except that you are the thread and so you are the story
And it's your story and it's all over now.'

'Thank you,' I said, 'And the two red spiders
Are still fighting each other in the corner
And I was so afraid that they would notice me and devour me
But they haven't while you were telling such a long story
And now I know they never will because yes I feel sleepy now.'

Serge

Come on, Serge, it's time to get up
Let go the bear, Mama's waiting
Come on, Serge, it's time, rub your eyes
Blow the hair off your face, it's morning
Look, the snow is falling
Look the jam is waiting, cherry, your favourite
Look, Papa's in pyjamas
Look, the sound is soft
Look, the sound lies heaped upon the ground
Look, the wolves are gone, your ankle isn't bleeding
It never was, Serge, you were dreaming

Nanny's here
Even if you can't see her, Mama can, Papa can't
One day you'll see me better
When the tubings are unplugged
When your ninety-seventh birthday becomes zero
When the snow stops falling
When there's white but no sky
When you pass through the window of the hospice
When your ankle feels the warmth of the wolf's breath,
Nanny's breath, Serge

You're my little angel
Blow your hair out of your eyes
Blow your eyes out of your hair
The curtains are flapping in the light
You won't need your bear any more
Time to get up
It's morning

Bear, with Teacup

They drank tea, they talked:
politics, people in the park,
pet dogs, beasts in the bedroom.
They ruminated, they regretted:
Servants (pregnant, drunk), children (in Berlin),
estates gone to seed, French this, French that.
The men remembered some disastrous woman.
The women remembered God knows whom.

One man listened, at his favourite table
at the Café Weber; and, for one moment—
I saw it! or was it in the Mirror?—
was consumed entire by a sheet of hellish flame.
It passed, but recurred,
each time a novel coming of it,
so masterful that Tolstoy's and Dostoyevsky's voices
crack like adolescents' in comparison.
The flame: his crippling modesty.

Is it possible for a genius to be lovable?
Turgenev.

The Holy One

When drunk, I saw the icon, it opened its doors and received me.
'Take me to Father Abraham and his trillion children,' I said,

'take me to rest my head among the stars and the grains of sand
      of the sea.'
'I am an icon,' said the icon, 'is there a candle burning in front of me?'

'Take me to the Lord Jesus who wears the red stole and who
      has a kind face,'
I said, 'take me to his Holy Mother and to the Holy Tekla at
      the right and left doors,

and I shall lean against their holy robes and I shall find peace there.'
'Let me tell you a story,' said the icon:

'One day the Lord Jesus was walking in the cellar
 and he saw me leaning up against the wall.

"Your wood is rotten, little icon," he said, "and you have been drinking.
I am a painter and I shall paint you." So, the Lord Jesus took
      out his brushes

and took onto himself the divine madness and made me as himself.'
'Thank you,' little icon,' I said. 'I have not finished,' said the icon,

'and so it is you whom I have received and who wear the red stole
and who have the kind face and whose Holy Mother stands at
      your right

and whose blessed companion the Holy Tekla stands at your left.'
'I am an icon,' I said to Father Abraham, 'is there a candle burning
      in front of me?'

'A trillion stars burn in front of you, little icon,' said Father Abraham,
'and your head rests among them and among all the grains of sand of
      the sea.

You have taken on the divine madness and the brushes under
      your red stole
are still wet with my tears.' 'And so I am home, Father Abraham,'
      I said.

'No,' he said, 'You are in the cellar as you will soon remember,
and you have been drinking, as is the way with painters who
      look for candles burning.'

Annie Fischer Playing Beethoven

For Cyprian

The first second
it sounds all wrong.
You listen longer you struggle
you but never she she just
proceeds.
Later along in the piece
every other artist's interpretation begins to sound
slightly off
then more than slightly.
Still longer along
something struggles hard
not you this time and never she she
just proceeds.
A door snaps open you are in the composer's brain endless
    rooms open up light up
in which you are
optional.
You grab for your glasses, a compass, the walls, your birth
    certificate, anything, while
she just proceeds

Eighty-eight keys

and all the pedals
are in every poem
of Emily Dickinson's
(most poems achieve
only a fraction of these).

They are all there.

That she sometimes chooses to strike
just one or none
and that repeatedly
that she sometimes chooses to press
just one or none
and that repeatedly
is her own affair.

Justinian

No, not the famous one. Just me. Reign of
Cincinnatus. Something transparent slipped.
Still in my mortal envelope, don't know why.
Banks of the Dee, bomb craters, sirens, flares,
fake airfields to fool Gerry, Chester
1940, a ridiculous number, really. I'm walking alright,
across the field, the flares, the smell of the estuary,
smell of rancid margarine. No hurry to cross.
The field seems as decent as any other.
My family must be asking 'Where's Justinian?
Everyone else got here.' This language's like glass,
yet I think in it. They said the Egyptians had glass.
We couldn't quite grasp what it was supposed to be, nor why.
'Just be good,' my mother said. That helps now, rather.
No hurry to cross this field. A gap's as good as a guess.
Gerry was always a bit strange, as was night.
Seems you've got both now for a while yet, Justinian.

November 12th

For Colin

So many young men went into the earth
In nineteen eighteen. No one remembers.
A million Brits, half a million Yanks, rotting
In Flanders fields. The old Lie. At Orléans,
The huge Cathédrale Sainte-Croix with its shrine
Stands empty. A few old plaques say 'Read me,'
And a few tourists do. One day a year,
More come. So many young men, some trusting,
Some really cool. Their letters home, their poems,
All but three of which no one remembers, rot.
In Paris, at the old Cinémathèque,
Two films by Gance, a silent and a talkie,
Also decay, *J'Accuse*, filmed twice for its
End—two million soldiers, dead, stinking, rise
From their fresh graves and march upon those still
Alive, us, accusing us of the supreme
War crime: stupidity; march over us,
While we are busily wasting the peace
Bought with their balls. '*J'acc* . . . .' 'Sorry, the film broke.'

'Let's go home. Look at the paper! Our leader
Of the moment says we'll fight. Complicated.
I don't know why but well we will and then
We'll know why. We'll send so many young men,
And young women, too, that's progress, and we'll
Remember why and know, like when that old
Archduke went down with the *Lusitania*.'

Hymn

Where do the souls on a battlefield go?
Home, where someone oblivious is washing dishes?
Nowhere, so they can mourn their fallen mates?
Back to the morning,
because they have all the time in the world now
except the future? To the desks of their heads of state
to say 'You fancy cowards, if it was that important,
why weren't you out with us here this day?'

And the wind blows 'I love you, honey' and 'you fancy cowards'
like stardust
to the farthest stars.

The Mahogany Desk

Move away from the mahogany desk Leo stop writing those thin
sheets of paper blow out the blue candle can't you hear the threads
snapping red green black can't you feel the light shooting
through you lighting up your veins your arms your bald forehead
your bad skin your beautiful spine your wrinkles can't you hear the sand
blowing through the room Pharaoh's scribes are coming for you Leo
they're going to take you from me they're going to make you
a scribe unto Pharaoh you'll live in a small brick house you'll write accounts
you'll write prayers you'll be because all who can write well are part of
Pharaoh himself a kidney or a lung and there'll be no more Leo just the
immensity of sands sliding down the sides of dunes at night because
Pharaoh is all the sands that ever were he's that immense oh Leo run out of
the room play golf play gin rummy listen to Brahms go for a drive they're
coming for you oh why did you have to be so intelligent Pharaoh's
scribes wouldn't have taken you and I can't love
the mahogany desk and little blue candle the way you used to daddy.

Gone Fishing

My father cast a line deep in the silver
Layers of Lake Catherine, Wisconsin. 'Bill, were
He here . . . ,' he said, of his Uncle Bill, friend
And fishing mate from the 'thirties, whose end
Was to come in a fireball jet crash. He,
My father, wore a wide-brimmed straw hat. We
Stupidly thought it would protect his face
From skin cancer which, red, white, piece by piece,
Had already eaten up half his nose
And, as years tugged, tugged, would devour his dose
Of choked life outside-in. But then, the silver
Layers took the line deep, deeper still, the whirr
Of reel and rod the only sound, rowboat
Oars floating in conspiring silence. 'Float
Your line, Dick,' he said, as the layers of silver
Depths reflected noon light from the lake's salver
Straight into his oblivious pores, two twigs
Holding, in a summer rowboat, two twigs;
Two pasty worms, in a summer rowboat,
Who'd just gouged worms on hooks—the big hook (ought
They not have seen it?) poised over them, silver
Glinting, merciless, slow. The big kill, for
My father, came in stages, hook sunk deep,
Deeper, deepest in his silver soul; sleep,
Skin, smell ripped from his gills—sweet Christ! the waste
Of it—but that's the nineteen-eighties. Haste
We back to 'fifty-three, to dad and tad
In a rowboat on Lake Catherine, its pad
Of silver, like mirrors, flat, smooth, a speck
Of wood and worms floating thereon. I speak
Of it seldom now, only when answering
'Is your father around?' I say, 'Gone fishing.'

Lilac Time

The death of the mother.

Then comes the crack-up.

Jesus was spared
something, at least.

Bait

You turned a corner inside the little rowboat
and burst into a million colours.
I thought we were on a fishing trip.
I thought we were in a rowboat.
I thought I knew who you were.
At any rate who you had been.
My father: hat, face, rod, oars,
jokes, wounds, lunch box, insect repellent.

You turned a corner and through you
I could see so clearly the white light and all the stones
at the bottom of the lake.
No, not Lake Madeleine.
The universe, which is a lake, and now I knew it had a bottom.
Through you I could so clearly see
webby spongy hands, angelfish and crabs bigger than the Eagle Galaxy,
all walking slowly backwards on the bottom.

As if you had been
the glass woman in the science museum with her veins blue, arteries red,
and nerves the colour of every fear I had.

Something about empty boathouses along a shore.
Losing one's job. Trips to the dentist.
Divorce. Skin operations. Psychiatrists. Being caught
under a tree in the rain on a golf course
and hoping to be struck by lightning, and not,
and hoping I wouldn't notice—as lightning struck
the neon sign over the ninth hole in the distance
and everything went Ray Bradbury pink.

Just as you stooped to pick up more bait from the bucket. The real you.

Bait. What was really under
the faded yellow tee shirt, the clean jeans, the broken nose,
    the soft socks,
the hands, the watery blue eyes that you hadn't minded giving to me.

Bait. A ceaseless attracter of spasms of love, of spasms of hunger,
that the spasms of God know all the time, me this once, you never.

O Scene Changer!—sometimes You forget
to include the amnesia.

I am born

For my father

All the machines were turned off
Except the light, which at night
Is a machine. If the telephone rang,
Someone would answer it quickly
Saying 'Not now. He's in the middle
Of the death of Dora,' and hang up deftly,
Not to stop the flow, the sputter,
The chronic confidence, the grand expanse
 (Because, normally, you were inward,
A black clawlike ingrown nail),
The care of your reading out loud.
We would sit back in our chairs,
Or on the sofa, and take it all in:
The whiteness of the whale; ambergris;
All that great heart lying still;
Reader, I married him; it was the best of times;
I wasted time and now time wastes me;
Even once, the opening of the Joseph tetralogy,
But that was curtailed, admiration
Not being an acceptable substitute for love.
And it was love, Lee, that you kayaked us
Down the river of, madly, expertly,
We all hilariously packed in side by side,
Tilted, screaming with pleasure
(Silently, of course) as the course
Of your voice embraced us.   Only when
You paused for breath could I hear
The digging under the rug, under the planks,
Deep, it seemed, under the house.
Could moles, I thought, be scraping with
Their razor paws, up through the dirt,
Just to hear you?   I would have.
Blind things, anyway, digging upwards.

Once, I thought, you heard it, too; when you
Winced at Marlow with Kurtz's fiancée—
But who wouldn't have winced at that?
Just to hear you, most of us with
Eyes closed, to squeeze the maximum
Of beauty from your sandpaper voice;
And to best be in that house of blessed refuge
Whose name is Being Read To.
Scrapes, scrapes. Scratches below the basement.
But why talk of ambulances? Not then. Not yet.
It was the best of times.

Crow Crossing Street

Earlier today I saw a crow crossing the street.
Avenue de Tourville. It took its time.
Buses, mopeds, bikes—not many, it's true, but even so.
It felt like doing it. So, it did it.

Very short, crows. Not more than nineteen centimeters.
Not even halfway high as the hub of a steel bike spoke.
Not that it cared. It did look up now and then,
the way anyone crossing a street looks up and around,

especially on brilliant days. Tall, I thought,
is not anywhere in the scale of values of a crow.
There it was, crossing near the rest of us. No, it wasn't sick.
Careful, of course. Bright, shiny. A high stepper.

Were we, in its shiny eyes, blobby baby brontosauruses?
Did the macadam feel no different from the congealed magma
so familiar to the feet of the first crows? Were the
cars and bikes whizzing by no different—to its shiny eyes—

from Thoth or copper-footed Mercury or angels
when they whizzed across sand, swamp, jungle, temple?
Of course, those whizzers knew what they were whizzing across—
crows' turf—so they were one up on us, as usual.

I wondered as I walked, was it as hard for this crow
to cross the street, not fly, as it would be for us to try to fly,
not cross? No, I thought. Which is why this planet is its,
not ours, no matter how many Tourvilles we paste all over it.

Sunflower

The Martian in the garden is the sunflower.

Taller than you.
But who are you when there is the sunflower?

Instead of a brain a hundred black eyes like seeds squeezed shut
A twitch of yellow thumb stubs around it.
Not enough stem.
That's all there is
Of the sunflower.

It does not see the sun.
It feels the heat of what could be the sky.
    heatrise   heatnoon   heatset
It follows the each beat of that heat as the only heart
It has.

It remembers the day all night,
Since night is only a library
To the sunflower.

And if the sunflower were
To have its own brain and heart?

It would eat you or rule you.
Because who are you when there is the sunflower?

Doctor, My Dear

In the middle of a field the Irish are so fond of:
Something like a spiral in the burnt grass.
Someone held my arm in a grip of steel,
Stopping me from walking further or from following
The rings within the bigger rings and beyond them
To the mountains that ringed the rings and needed no more name.
Two women in white were walking arm in arm through the
Burnt yellow grass, tall slender women as from before the Great War,
Long muslin columnar dresses, gloves, veiled hats, graceful women
Who had been raised in grace and had known not what abuse
And so were the gladder to talk to each other undisturbed,
As if the yellow grass were the sands of the sea of the beach at Skagen
And I the red setting sun, I not luminous but a red path
Over the lapping waters that, too, did not wish to disturb them.
Sisters? I thought. Mother and daughter, finely grown?
Something in myself that I had never seen and that the spiral showed,
Which is why I was stopped from following? Can we have,
Inside our thick blind ox-like brutal wrestlers' ribs,
Something so bridal as this? I think it is so,
Doctor, my dear. You throw us off our motorbikes
As you did Lawrence of Arabia and for one second only
We see the real macadam.

Elgar

He rests under the grass.
In his music—ours now even in cities—the mown hay,
The ripple of bluebells, the skirting of white clouds,
The, yes, dark spots, the freshness of a child's notice
And an old man's gift for the fatness of tone of the thrush.
In his music, the pulse of the wrist, the eager leap of the
Heart. Here lies . . . what? No. Never.
Here lies who. Here lies the humid earth,
The, ignored by most, who of it. And Who made it.
And, in our ears, thanks to that young man,
The breathing of it. He knew the secret
Of which we have grown ashamed: that beauty
Carries us, of hope, of grandeur, of
Nothing very much, of even less than that,
Before and not too long after destruction
By the usual destroyers. That beauty is, must be—
Must!—memory. The field aches to move backwards,
And (can you hear it?) does. This he knows,
Even in sleep, the earth of him. In ours, do we?

Antigone

I've come to bury my brother.
I never would put him in a warm bed,
Now I put him in a cold one.

He has already rotted because he is earth,
But earth is never rotten so I have come to put him in it,
To leave him on it is indecent.

The stars shift,
The earth shifts,
And in between
Is a privilege.

My brother was obnoxious, but he breathed.
I who am breaking the law by burying my brother
Am breathing,
Which is all I hear.

Any form of breath has value, given its source,
Even my when he was breathing hateful brother,
Even the judges who condemn him to rot,
Even I the always ugly one.

I did not know this yesterday, I know it now.

When we forget the breathing of our brother,
We become all of us dangerous.

So I have come to ask mercy of my brother,
But he is not here, he has shifted with the stars.
I am therefore doing the next best thing that is like love:
I have come to bury my brother.

The important thing about love is not that it may be eternal
But that it can be retroactive.
It is not eternity that brings me here this night.
Tell that to your lawyers in the morning.

Hope finishes

Hope finishes last
in the race but the rest of
the runners are dead.

Goldberg Variations

Don't knock insomnia.
It produced the Logos, humility, and the *Goldberg Variations*.

All the horror that enters the world
does so after
a good night's sleep.

Satan
sleeps like a top.

Oracle

In the middle of a slum I saw a
Rainbow of solid emerald and this
I could not understand. I saw women
Beaten up and some men too cowering in
Flats and children trashed, unwanted and
Wanted ones, and not enough money and
Too much money and spiral-bound projects
In boardrooms. 'This I understand,' I said,
'Why am I being shown it?' A voice
From the navel said, 'You understand it
As little as the rainbow. Both are, as
That teacher over there, who has begun
To talk to herself on kerbs, knows and
Works with daily.'

Rolling Back the Stone

I passed some time in Egypt.
I was two or twenty-two, I don't remember which;
Certainly not thirty-two, which is when the real work began.
My mother was irritable there, my father was as always.

I remember pomp and sweat and animated dust.
I remember also suffocation with one hidden chamber of air,
Which was art. I remember traffic and laughter,
Which was life. And I liked that life, in Egypt.

If the camel had had the least interest in anything
Outside of itself, it would have taken up the offer
Of dominion over the garden. Instead that honour
Went to the lesser baby, who was greedy and stood ready.

I found a well in Egypt, in the middle of the loquacious sands.
(My hearing has always been good.) I drank liberally from it.
Thus are bargains struck. Such water does not come cheaply,
And I was glad to pay, but not in Egypt.

Maybe Egypt was not Egypt.
Maybe the water was not water.

All I know is that when I came to, this morning,
Against the eternal relief that bird chirps provide,
I found myself in an even stranger garden
Than the strange lost first.

For one moment, before joy struck me senseless,
I thought I was two or twenty-two again and back in Egypt.
At odd moments even now,
I am almost disappointed not to be.

Nicodemus

I seek you at night because one talks better at night
I seek you in secret because I am afraid
I seek you in silence so as not to break the hope
I seek you in whispers because the loud are always wrong
You as the worse insomniac receive me kindly

Your words to me do not relate to my questions
They are whiskey without the addiction
Forgiveness without explanation
Truth in full sedition

I cannot see your face nor you mine
Which is the best mercy
The small hours offer
To those like me who teach for a living
In the lesser light of the morning

I am sorry that neither your murderers nor followers
Ever think to pay you
This kind of visit

'Her band of gold always caught the light'

Today I opened an envelope
sent by my cousin Elizabeth
from Ringgold, Georgia, USA.
Elizabeth indicates rather than
writes, never more than two dozen words—
rose petals, some dried, some fresh, all fragrant.
Out fell an article of hers, top of
page 5A, the *Rolla Daily News*,
26 June 2007:
'Her band of gold always caught the light,'
a reminiscence of her late mother Lillian,
my aunt whom I had never met.
There she was, a photo of her
circa 1936, atop
Elizabeth's not more than two hundred words—
a strong young woman emerging from
shadow, the head tilted slightly down,
a half smile, thick beautiful brown eyebrows,
a broad forehead kind and troubled and kind.
The left hand rested near the shoulder
of the black dress. On one finger the ring
that her husband Jack had given her,
yes, caught the light, as it later did
when (Elizabeth writes) Lillian
would play piano for her children—
the ring lost now (Elizabeth writes),
meaning, is somewhere unknown.

An article in a newspaper—
local news as befits the universe—
about things lost and found and lost,
about Lillian, about Elizabeth's
late husband Myron (another love match),
about human dignity, about

the dignity of so-called things.
Reading it, seeing the photos (one, too,
of Elizabeth and Myron
finding something that had been immured
for a hundred years in an old shack,
a pair of glasses a carpenter
had left on a support brace), one was
less ashamed of the human condition.

Tomorrow, I shall fold the story
in four, so that it shows only
the photograph of Lillian.
I shall frame it and put it on my wall
for daily seeing, for knowing that
some leave the world a better place than
they found it, or try. And I think that
my wall will say, 'Me, too, now.'

Four days ago I thought of Harry,
twenty years my senior, my first real
friend, dead in 1975,
and with him the thought that of one's first
real friend—and here I mean, first; real; friend—
one could say 'He sank deep into the soft wax
of my capacity to love.'
I had half-forgotten it, until
Lillian and Jack and my father
and Myron and the carpenter and
my wife and Harry and my mother
and that astonishing rest
came tumbling out of an envelope
from a cousin in Ringgold Georgia
who notices what catches the light.

At Evening

For Raymond

We have lit, my dear Socrates, the candles,
And our wives are at their support group,
And we have gathered—Critias, Hermocrates,
And I, and the wise old man who took the hemlock
And who has kindly agreed to come in place
Of Cratylus who is ill—to tell you that we have discussed
Among ourselves, as you had requested, what topic
We should present to you this evening
For our entertainment, since we had so handsomely,
So you said, entertained you with our discourses
On what you had set forth at that time—
When you explained that we are all made up
Of little bright blue triangles, and the universe as well,
And how amid the moving mud and the moving glister
Our souls yearn toward the Good, and that
Through discipline and humility and love,
We can contemplate, beyond the brightest gods,
Goodness, in the swing and stasis of eternity.
And so we asked ourselves this morning, what topic?
And this is what we present to you now:
Entertain us on the topic of the Good.

There is a breath that lifts the triangles,
And, in the lifting, music.
There is, beyond the plucky wings
Or exhausted wings of souls,
Beyond the brightest of the bright gods,
Beyond the Good, a Clown in tears.
I did not, therefore—I was wrong,
My dear Timaeus—contemplate the Good.
Our concern is to comfort the Clown,
And as we try, in our clumsy way,
We become almost as young as He.

And then we take, oh such a long nap
In the evening which is the dawn,
Knowing that our efforts did, somewhat,
Comfort. And nothing is better than that.
And in our nap we hear,
Certainly not from Saïs or from Athens,
Unfamiliar words to me:
'Rest in peace. Rest in peace.'
And we do. I was not expecting that.

The Good Man Asleep in His Chair

For Paul

There is a certain trust in sleep.
The asleep are so defenceless, with their mouths open and
   their necks back,
Their hands slack, holding neither weapons nor flowers.

The only thing that holds him, then—breathing or God.
Though his living room is his, it is not his now.
Though his chair is his chair, he has no hold over it.
He has loosed the cords, his wife and children out somewhere,
His wristwatch unwatched, his hairy legs stretched into the carpet.
He owns nothing now, yet sleeps as if he owns everything.
And, as he is a good man, he does.

With biscuit

They talked on of the dead, of someone's mother with the red hair,
of how she had been as a girl or said she had been. Of Stevie
    died so young
and of the words he had never been able to pronounce properly
and of if he could say them correctly now in heaven.
Of old Sister Mary Margaret; hilarious. Of a chubby child—
me, I wondered?—but I'm not chubby, far from it—
Ruthie, are you fine with that biscuit?—but fine is for weather
so didn't know what to answer down here—and before I could speak
chubby child was back again talked of in their midst
and I not there for them because I was not the dead.

They talked on of last week's party, if Yvon had really walked out,
of how Margaret—yes, you Margaret—had lost the plot,
but then turned out she hadn't, nothing obscene at all,
just a yoga position demonstrated on the rug.
Of how Uncle Carl's food had come through his nose, only it
    hadn't, really—
how'd you do that then, Carlie?—and it seemed to me that this too
was talking of the dead: Margaret last week, Carl last week,
Mum shopping when the ice cream bin fell and broke her foot,
Carl way up over me talking of then and so not seeing me now.

The proportion's all off, can't we ask me can't we ask us about now?
About how your feet are hurting? About why I'm so skinny?
About whether to shut the windows right this second
lest the wind east wind very very cold east wind
blow us back to where there's Stevie saying toatser, I mean, toaster.

Then the moon came up, and we all were looking at it,
and so the dead disappeared for a while.

About the author

RICHARD W. HALPERIN has seen over 100 of his poems published in journals, mainly in Ireland and the U.K. since he started sending them out in 2005. He has appeared frequently in issues of *Cyphers, Revival, THE SHOp, Poetry Ireland Review* and *The Stony Thursday Book*, and was *The Stinging Fly*'s featured poet in the summer of 2009. 'For Victor Gollancz' won first prize in the 2007 Blue Butterfly Christian Poetry Competition, Inverurie Scotland. He gave his first readings at Glenstal Abbey and at Glencree Centre for Reconciliation, followed by readings at festivals in Bantry and Athlone, and in venues such as the Dublin Writers' Centre, the Dundalk Writers' Circle and the Live Poets Society, Paris. Mr. Halperin holds a Ph.D. in English Literature from the City University of New York. Until 2005 he was chief of teacher education for the United Nations Educational, Scientific and Cultural Organization (UNESCO), Paris, which entailed travel and work in Asia, Africa and Central and Eastern Europe. For UNESCO, he edited the downloadable book *Reading and Writing Poetry: The Recommendations of Noted Poets from Many Lands on the Teaching of Poetry in Secondary Schools*, available in English, French and Spanish versions. *Anniversary* is Mr. Halperin's debut collection.

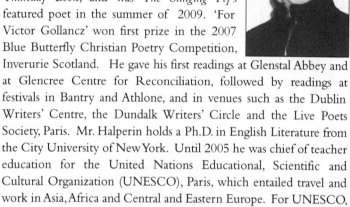

Photo: Lukas Ambry